— Gracie Kay —

THE
BREAKING
AND
MAKING
OF
ME

The Breaking And Making Of Me
How to Survive, be Revived and Thrive in the Face of the Ultimate Betrayal
Copyright © 2018 Gracie Kay

All Rights Reserved. No part of this book may be used or reproduced in any manner whatsoever without written permission except in the case of brief quotations embodied in critical articles and reviews.

For information, contact:

Studio Griffin
A Publishing Company
studiogriffin@outlook.com
www.studiogriffin.net

Cover Design by Ruth E. Griffin
Image by © bramgino/Adobe

Illustrations by Gracie Kay and Ruth E. Griffin

Unless otherwise indicated, all Scripture taken from New King James Version Second Edition. Copyright © 1995, 2006 by Thomas Nelson, Inc.

Scripture quotations marked KJV taken from The Holy Bible, King James Version. New York: American Bible Society: 1999.

Scripture quotations marked NIV taken from the Holy Bible, New International Version®. Copyright © 1973, 1978, 1984 International Bible Society. Used by permission of Zondervan. All rights reserved. The "NIV" and "New International Version" trademarks are registered in the United States Patent and Trademark Office by International Bible Society. Use of either trademark requires the permission of International Bible Society.

Scripture quotations marked AMP taken from The Amplified Bible, Copyright 1954, 1958, 1962, 1964, 1965, 1987, by the Lockman Foundation. All rights reserved. Used by permission.

First Edition

ISBN-13: 978-1-954818-06-4

1 2 3 4 5 6 7 8 9 10

DEDICATION

To my Lord and Savior without whom I would not be the woman I am today. To my parents for their unfailing love and support. To my cousin and my best friend for their listening ears, shoulders to cry on, and hearts that understood. To my many close friends for their fierce support and constant prayers. To my therapist and my doctor whom the Lord placed in my life to provide the right kind of help. To all of my readers, may your hearts be touched and inspired, and may you survive your journey and emerge stronger!

CONTENTS

Author's Note	1
Introduction	3
Moments	5
Step One	21
Step Two	25
Step Three	31
Step Four	37
Step Five	41
Step Six	49
Step Seven	57
Step Eight	81
Step Nine	89
Conclusion	95
Acknowledgements	101
About the Author	103

AUTHOR'S NOTE

Ever since I was a little girl, I dreamed of writing children's books, romance novels, poetry; anything to inspire others. Never in my wildest dreams did I imagine the pages of this book would contain the most intimate and life changing battles of my life! I was asked by a friend, "If you could do anything with 100% certainty and not fail, what would it be?" My immediate response was, "write." So, it is my hope that my story and my journey with the Lord will inspire and help other women who find themselves in similar situations. I am no Lysa TerKeurst, or Priscilla Shirer, but I am a treasured daughter of the Lord. May He use me to offer you hope!

Gracie Kay

INTRODUCTION

I am Gracie Kay, and at one point, not long ago, I thought I had the perfect life. It was what every little girl pictures her life will be. I had a family, a career and a loving husband. While involved in my church and my community, I truly felt God had blessed me abundantly. Then one day, without warning, my world came crashing down around me. My perfect picture of a family was broken into pieces. I was suddenly faced with an adulterous spouse, a crumbling marriage, and shattered dreams. I didn't even begin to know how to put it all back together... How was I to survive the ultimate betrayal? How would I put the pieces of my life back together and move on? All I wanted to do was just survive what was happening around me. I wanted my heart, my dreams, and my life to be revived. I wanted my life to thrive and to prosper.

I learned that to do this, I must find grace and comfort in my Lord and Savior Jesus Christ. Please join me on my journey from a broken past to a new, meaningful life. Discover how the steps I took can help your broken heart heal and help you on your own journey of forgiveness and healing.

Gracie Kay

MOMENTS

What are the moments that make up our individual lives? There are many singular moments in our lives that affect us: our first kiss, our first serious boyfriend, or sweet sixteen. Our college graduation, our wedding day, the birth of a child, or maybe the loss of a loved one. It could even be a fateful phone call, a job relocation, or news from the doctor you never thought you'd hear.

These events, when examined by themselves, typically only change us for a season, or short-term period of our life. However, when woven together into the fabric of our lives, they serve to change our destiny. As I glimpse into the past, these are the moments that were life changing instances in time... A chance meeting... A near death experience... and, My wedding day. These are the three special moments I've chosen to share with you, and they are just a fraction of my story.

Moment One... A Chance Meeting

It was the second semester of my junior year in high school. I had just been through a horrible break up because I refused to give up my virginity outside of marriage. So, like most teenage girls I did the only thing I knew how to do: I got up, I got dressed to impress, and I fixed up my outward appearance to mask the rejection I felt inside. Little did I know what the Lord had in store right around the next corner! Literally, as I turned the corner of the east wing, I came face-to-face with Troy, one of my older brother's friends. He was tall, dark, and handsome with black hair, dimples, and tan skin. I can still remember the striped polo shirt and jeans he was wearing that day. He took one look at me and could tell I had been crying. He cupped my chin with his hand, looked deep in my eyes and said, "you deserve better." I don't remember if I actually said anything or if I simply smiled and scampered down the hall to my next class with a smile on my face. You may or may not believe in love at first sight, but for me that's what it was. God placed him in my path at the exact time I needed him. This moment changed my life forever! A few weeks later we started dating.

Moment Two... A Near Death Experience

Christmas morning, 1995. I felt like a pretty cool gal driving my dove gray 1990 Mustang LX 5.0. I was headed down a back road less than a mile from my house. Troy was right behind me in his red Nissan truck. We had just left my house: he was going to work, and I was on my way to be in my first parade. It was my senior year and I had the honor of serving on the Belk Teen Fashion Board. We modeled clothes in fashion shows, represented Belk Department store in parades, and appeared at local community events. I was filled with excitement and anticipation! Then BAM! It all changed in the blink of an eye. I still don't know what happened. I pulled out from a stop sign and saw a glimpse of white. I swerved off the road, over corrected, and ended up wrapped around a tree. It happened so fast, I didn't have time to react. Poor Troy saw the whole thing happen. But our great and mighty God was with me and protected me from harm. You see, that tree I crashed into landed mere inches from my head. If I wasn't such a petite gal, I probably wouldn't be here today. But it was in that moment that Troy realized he loved me - when he almost lost me!

Moment Three... My Wedding Day

February 2000, less than a month after a record-breaking snowstorm hit North Carolina. We had been pummeled with twenty-four inches of snow that paralyzed parts of our state for weeks. But, this day dawned bright and glorious. It was an unusual sixty-nine degrees in the middle of February. Our families, Troy, and myself had been preparing for this day for over a year and a half. Our wedding day! Like any bride, I was blushing and adorned with the perfect gown. I had chosen a sleeveless dress with a sweetheart neckline and miles of tulle and lace. I wore satin gloves and my grandmother's diamond bracelet.

As I nestled my arm into the crook of my dad's arm, he asked, "Are you sure you want to do this sweetheart? It's not too late... you can still turn around."

I turned and smiled at my dad and gently laughed. "I've never been surer of anything in my life! God choose him for me."

The church doors opened, and I walked down the aisle to chords of Cannon and D. I can still picture him standing at the altar. He looked handsome and debonair in his black tuxedo. I saw a tear slip out of the corner of his eye as he beamed at me. We had written our own vows; and the ceremony that followed was exactly what I had dreamed it would be: perfect! I knew in my heart I would love this man forever no matter what life chose to throw our way!

One More Moment... Moment Four

Fast forward sixteen years, three houses, and three kids later. It was a few days after my birthday. A Friday in early April. I was out of town trying to finish the most critical professional project of my life. I had just checked out of the hotel and was walking along the streets of a quaint little town about an hour from my home. Troy called, and I wanted to talk about birthday plans for the evening, but I noticed his voice was distant and moody. I asked him what was wrong, but I was not prepared for what followed. That phone call changed the course of my life and my future.

These four moments outline the events that led to the beginning of my marriage with Troy and to the beginning of that same marriage which I was no longer sure of. Everything in between could be considered ordinary in comparison. The moments following were once unthought of and now what defines me as a person. My journey will map these out.

Gracie Kay

THE BREAKING

Sometimes God allows an event to occur in our lives to wake us up and help us reevaluate everything and everyone we hold dear. This event helps us examine our lives. To break us down in order to mold us into the woman we should have been all along! The phone conversation Troy and I had on the street corner that day was the event that broke my fantasy world into pieces, and amazingly it wasn't about infidelity. Not yet!

At this point, I had no idea what was really going on. What I thought was a happy marriage now seemed to only be a fantasy. Troy told me he was unhappy with every area of our life. And as if that wasn't enough, he made me promise not to share our problems with anyone. I knew something was wrong, but I believed him. I trusted him 100% because I never had a reason not to.

Needless to say, I was blindsided by the admission.

In football, blindsided is when the other team's players do not notice a play because their view is obscured by other players around them. Talk about hindsight being 20/20 or perfectly clear. I had been focused on my career, my kids and our busy life. My vision had been obscured and I didn't notice the play that was being made in the background!

I had noticed for months he was moody, distant and ill. I assumed it was the stress of his job and the number of hours he worked. Boy, was I wrong. Over the course of our hour-long conversation, harsh words, and many tears later I learned he "wasn't happy." He wasn't happy with me, our marriage, our level of intimacy, our church, his job…basically our whole lives. My perfect world came crashing down around me. It is only by God's grace and protection that I made the hour-long trip home. I was crushed in every way imaginable. I could see my life breaking into a million pieces right before my eyes and I was powerless to stop it!

I'm sure many of you reading this right now are fixers by nature. As women, we are used to fixing our kid's problems, fixing dinner, fixing our husband's lunch, and just plain out trying to solve all the world's problems from our own little corner. So, of course, that was my first step. After picking myself up off the floor and trying to regain my emotions, I started making a list. How could I "fix" the problems in my marriage? I couldn't control my husband's thoughts and feelings, but I could change things I was doing. So, I started attacking things on that list with fervent intent. "Okay Lord," I'd pray. "I am doing my part, now open my husband's eyes."

I've always considered myself a strong, Christian woman and have strived to live according to His ways. But let me tell you something ladies, trying to "fix" my marriage didn't work. I did everything I could possibly think of to help close the gap and change his feelings. Nothing worked, and things just kept getting worse. He was working longer and longer hours. He was short-tempered. He was unkind and void of emotion towards me. He wanted to spend less and less time with the kids and I. As the months passed, I kept questioning him. I was trying to figure out what was going on inside his head. The answers were always the same. "I'm tired. I'm stressed with work. I regret turning down that job offer and now I'm stuck. Just give me time. You're trying too hard to fix things."

I started feeling as though we were roommates and not husband and wife. We were living separate lives in the same house. I was working full time, keeping the house clean, and raising our kids. He worked and did whatever he wanted to do in his free time. Deep in my heart I had a feeling I was losing him, but I didn't understand why. We had been together for twenty-two years, married for sixteen. I had loved this man since I was young and couldn't imagine my life without him! There was no reason not to trust him and just wait for him to wake up and realize how blessed we were.

But over the next four months he continued to grow more distant. My prayers started taking a turn. I begged God to protect my children but do whatever He had to do to me to wake my husband up.

One Saturday in August, after an argument and an emotional conversation, Troy said it might be best if we took some time apart. I told him I didn't agree, and it wouldn't solve anything. The next morning, he left early for a run. He had done the same thing every Sunday for four months. I couldn't take it anymore, so I sat and wrote him a letter. I poured out my heart and shared with him my feelings and my fears. I left it laying on his dresser where I knew he would find it. Later, when it was gone, I knew he had it, but he never spoke a word about it.

The next day in church, Troy was distant and pushed my hand away when I tried to reach for him. That afternoon while he was taking a nap I decided to look for the letter. I wanted to see if he had thrown it away or kept it. I opened his wallet and saw a piece of paper folded over. My heart immediately warmed because I thought he had enough compassion and love for me to keep the letter I had written to him, tucked away safe in his wallet where he could take it out and look at it over and over again. I felt a glimmer of hope for the first time in months. I took out the paper and opened it.

It was a love letter written to Troy by another woman who didn't even have the guts to sign it! My heart FELL to my feet! The breath left my body and I had to keep myself from throwing up. You see that piece of paper was not my handwriting. It was worn, and I could tell it had been in his wallet for months. I can still recall the words almost word for word, but I could never share them with anyone.

With my heart throbbing in my chest, I called him to our bedroom. He could tell from the look on my face something was terribly wrong. I patted the hope chest next to me and handed him the letter. My voice trembled with emotion as I said, "Please tell me this isn't what I think it is."

He held it for a moment, then wadded it up and said, "I have no idea what it is." I told him I was looking for my letter when I saw it in his wallet. He continued to deny it was his and he didn't know how it got there. In that moment, I knew the person sitting beside me was no longer the man I married. I could no longer trust him. But, to his face I said, "You are my husband and if you are telling me the truth then I believe you."

I spent hours that evening agonizing about how to find out the truth. Conversations of the past few days kept playing over and over in my mind. You see, the kids and I had been on a road trip and we had not seen Troy for nine days. We had returned home three days prior and he was so happy to see the kids. He had gone on a trip himself and had brought them back presents. However, he didn't bring anything for me and he didn't want to even look or talk to me. I felt no love from my husband. He was talking about wanting to take time away from me and now the letter. What was happening? The pieces began to fall into place in my mind, but my heart refused to see.

The next morning, our son was scheduled for oral surgery. Troy said he couldn't take off work, so my mom went with me. While we were sitting in the waiting room I looked over at my mom with tears in my eyes and said, "I can no longer trust the man I married. What should I do?"

She simply said, "Check your phone bill and you will get the answer you are looking for."

It only took a few moments for me to see the same phone number appear multiple times a day. I picked up my phone and searched for the number in my contacts. A name I knew very well! In that moment, I knew my life would never be the same. Emotions flooded my soul; anger, disbelief, denial, rage, sadness, despair and even hate! Yes, ladies, even a woman of faith can feel these things and it is totally natural. You see it is usually someone close and this person wasn't just an acquaintance, but someone I considered a friend. The betrayal went even further. Our children were friends. We saw each other on a daily and weekly basis. She even helped me with that major professional project I had completed all those months earlier. In fact, she even suggested I go out of town and spend time by myself to help focus and think through things. Little did I know it was just a ploy to get me out of the way.

My mother was so sweet and kind and told me not to jump to conclusions immediately. She encouraged me to control the anger and to discuss things with my husband before immediately accusing him. To give him a chance to explain. A few hours later, after I got my son back home and settled down, I got on the computer. I studied the phone bill and began adding up the minutes and hours he had talked to her. I saw how many times a day and started putting dates and times and places together. With every piece to the puzzle I became more and more enraged. You see I only looked at the one month, but the amount of time he spoke to her added up to seven and a half days. That's how much time he had stolen from me and our children. I couldn't bear to look back at the past months because I knew what I'd find. This was not a simple one-night stand or a fleeting relationship. I knew because of his actions from the last four months and how turned upside down our relationship had been. But how much worse could it be? Questions were spinning through my mind. Was he in love with her? He had been so mean and hateful to me. How could I be so stupid? How did I not know? She was my friend, my colleague, and someone I trusted. How could she do this to me? How could she do this to her family as well? How did this happen? It took all I could not to call and reach out to her in anger and give her a piece of my mind.

Then I heard the pastor's voice from our sermon the day before. "Be angry and sin not." I knew I had to rise above my anger and be the bigger person. But let me tell you ladies, that was the last thing I wanted to do. When he finally arrived home that evening I was sitting in the bedroom floor waiting. I had the phone bill printed and highlighted along with notes everywhere. At first, he tried to deny everything, saying it was just an emotional affair until I picked up his phone and played voice messages from her and shoved them in his face. You see, while he had been taking a nap I noticed he had saved messages on his phone. When I listened to them I heard her voice. I wanted to throw up after hearing her vulgar words and comments to him. There are some things you can never forget listening to. There was no denying the kind of relationship they had. Questions came spewing out of my mouth and the tears flowed freely. He begged for my forgiveness and I immediately gave in to him. I have always been a forgiving person by nature and I really believed in that moment he was sorry. Despite the circumstances and what he had done, I still loved him so very much.

However, in the coming months I would discover that forgiveness is a journey. Discovering the affair was just the beginning. My heart was shattered, and my marriage was in pieces. Everything that I had believed in was a lie. Up until this point the only thing I knew was that my husband was unhappy with our marriage and had committed adultery. But, I unknowingly would continue to be deceived for months to come. I thought I could forgive and forget, but it would not be quite that easy. How do you put a shattered heart back together? How do you piece a marriage and a family back together?

Shattered

Shattered means to be broken into many pieces. Danny Gokey has a song entitled "Tell Your Heart to Beat Again." All of these words describe a woman's world, a woman's life in aftermath of adultery. The songwriters talk about your life and your dreams being shattered into a thousand pieces. Your heart feels like it has stopped, and you don't know how to make it beat again! But you must put the past behind you, take a deep breath and move forward.

During the months prior to the discovery of the affair I was leading a broken life because I knew something in my marriage was broken. This lead to my heart being broken. After I discovered the affair my heart was no longer simply broken. My heart, my spirit, my marriage and my reality were all shattered. I felt like I was looking at my life through a thousand shattered pieces of my heart and I did not know how to begin the journey toward healing and becoming whole again.

Moving Forward

Every situation is unique. Whether you suspect adultery, have confirmed it, or have gone through it in the past everyone's situation is not the same and everyone will react in different ways. I pray my story will be an inspiration to all of you reading this. God has given me the strength to relive and share my story with all of you. I want you to learn how to survive, be revived, and to thrive in the face of the ultimate betrayal! Although, my level of "hell" has been more intense and lasted longer than I would ever thought possible, God has given me daily strength to make it through.

I want to begin by saying everything you think and feel in this moment is perfectly normal. My initial reaction was one of complete brokenness. My world was shattered and the life I had lived for the past seven months had been a lie. There was not a single memory, conversation, holiday, or date that was not tainted by his lies, deception, and betrayal. That first week I did not look back at phone calls and records, because I was trying so hard to forget and move on. But I wanted answers and he would not give them to me. When I say all my memories were tainted, I mean all of them. When I looked at the phone records more of the story was revealed. All day, every day for seven months. During an anniversary trip, on my birthday, Mother's Day, and even a family vacation. He was constantly engrossed in his phone texting and on social media. He never wanted to ride with the kids and I, but preferred to meet us at our destination instead. Suddenly it all made sense.

I fell into a deep depression and a black abyss. I couldn't stop crying. But, I had to do something. I had three kids depending on me and they did not need to see me fall apart. So, I made a choice.

I could sink further and further into the black hole, or I could decide to take steps to make my life better. My grandpa used to say that we make a choice about everything we do in life. What do you have the courage to choose? The steps I took may or may not be the same for you, but they helped turn my life around and set me on the right course.

Steps in My Journey
There are many roads and many paths to take in life. With each choice we make, with each step we take we are propelled towards our Destiny. Every day we choose a path. One path will lead us forward

and all others will lead us back. The steps I am sharing with you are ones God gave me the wisdom and guidance to take. They are intended to be a guide for you in hopes that He will help you in the midst of a very difficult journey.

> *The Lord is near to those who have a broken heart,*
> *And saves such as have a contrite spirit.*
> *Psalm 34:18 (NKJV)*

I love this Psalm. Here the psalmist speaks of a "broken heart" and a "contrite spirit." A broken heart is experienced when someone else causes a break in a relationship with us. On the other hand, a contrite spirit results when we feel sorrow for having broken or caused a breach of trust with God or another human being. The woman who experiences a broken heart, in many ways, is a "victim." I was a victim of my husband's rejection and adultery. Regardless of the cause, the natural and typical feeling that follows is one of complete devastation. Your life has been shattered. Other emotions are quick to follow such as fear, loneliness and despair. In many ways a broken heart creates a broken spirit. If your spirit is broken, you may lose the will to live, to love, and to trust. I lost all of it! There were many dark days when I contemplated riding myself of the pain in the most final way possible. Every time, I would see my children's faces and God would speak softly to me. "What about them?" I love my kids, but I was no longer whole. How could I love them the right way, when I could not even love myself! I did not trust my husband, and he did not seem to have any interest in rebuilding trust or helping me heal. He was confused and lost, and our marriage was in complete chaos. We were living under the same roof but fought all the time. I decided to take the first step. Join me on my journey . . .

ঔ JOURNAL 03
Take a moment to jot down the beginning moments of your personal experience when you first began to notice a change in your marriage.

THE BREAKING AND MAKING OF ME

Gracie Kay

STEP ONE

Seek Medical Help

I was an emotional wreck and I felt like a basket case in front of my kids. I realized that I needed help. I made an appointment with my medical doctor. She was kind and caring and told me that adultery is treated like grief in the medical world. I had never faced anything like this before, but it made perfect sense. I was grieving over the loss of my marriage relationship and I didn't know if my life would ever be the same. She prescribed a medication that would help calm my nerves and stop the crying. As a Christian woman, I felt weak for needing to depend on medication, that my belief in Christ and leaning on His strength should be enough. However, after speaking with several Christian women I realized that the Lord provides doctors, therapist and other medical professionals in order to help us. I knew I needed to be strong for my kids, and if medication would keep me from crying every second of the day then I was okay with that for a short time. Your doctor will prescribe a course of treatment depending upon your needs.

Proverbs 11:14 says, *"Where there is no counsel, the people fall; But in the multitude of counselors there is safety." (NKJV)* God created all of us with certain needs: physical, emotional, intellectual, psychological and spiritual. According to Philippians 4:19 we know that God is ready and able to supply all of our needs and we can find His help through prayer, bible study, listening to the Holy Spirit, and from the counsel of Godly people. When any of our life needs are not being met, then mental anguish occurs. When this anguish disrupts our daily activities or damages our relationships, then we must seek counsel.

Some of you may be asking where do I turn? There are different professionals, people and organizations you can go to for help.

Medical Doctors are licensed to treat grief but only by prescribing medication for blood pressure and/or depression. I was very fortunate because my doctor is a Christian and someone whom I felt comfortable talking to. The day I walked into the doctor's office my blood pressure was 183/160 and I had already lost seven pounds. Extreme stress and emotions can take a toll on your health and your body. For months and months, I got sick every time I ate. I had migraines, loss of sleep, dizziness, chest pains, and a pain in my side that would not go away. After numerous tests it was determined it was all stress related. I encourage you to take care of yourself and pay attention to your body during your difficult time. Your medical doctor may also recommend you talk with a professional counselor, psychiatrist, or psychologist.

Psychiatrist Verses Psychologist

Psychiatrist are trained medical doctors. They can prescribe medications. Traditionally most of their time with patients is spent on medication management as a course of treatment. Psychologists focus extensively on psychotherapy and treating emotional and mental suffering in patients with behavioral intervention. Refer to www.allpsychologyschools.com for more information and to decide which one is right for you.

Counselors

Christian, or Faith Based counselors provide psychological support and counseling services. They combine theology and spirituality with theories of modern behavior science. In other words, they help you see things from a Biblical perspective and help you apply God's principles to your situation.

Work Programs

There are many professions that offer mental health wellness programs, or Employee Assistance Programs (EAPs). Check and see if your place of work offers such a program by contacting your human resource department. You would be surprised at what is available to you because your profession wants to ensure their employees are healthy both physically and mentally. I will forever be grateful to my profession for offering such a program which paid for counseling services for myself for several months. Help was and still is available to my spouse and also to my children through such a program.

Family Medical Leave

Due to my profession I knew that I would be unable to perform to the best of my ability without taking care of my physical and mental health first. This was a scary step for me, because as a mother I was so used to putting my children and my spouse first and I wasn't sure how to take care of myself. My doctor insisted that I have a modified work schedule in order to seek the professional help that was needed and to take care of myself. The Family Medical Leave Act entitles eligible employees of covered employers to take unpaid, job-protected leave. This leave can be taken for specified family and medical reasons. Health insurance coverage will still continue during this period as well. You can visit www.dol.gov to see the Employees Guide to the Family Medical Leave Act from the United States Department of Labor. Your human resource department will be able to tell you how to go about applying for Family Medical Leave and give you more specific information. My husband and I have used Family Medical leave with the birth of all of our children, numerous surgeries and the hospitalization of a child.

೧ JOURNAL ೧

How do you feel at this moment? Would you benefit from a medical doctor's help? How do you feel about a psychiatrist verses a psychologist?

_____

_____

_____

_____

_____

_____

_____

_____

Gracie Kay

STEP TWO

Find Your Support System

God's timing is never accidental, although sometimes it feels that way. You see my cousin had asked me to do an online Bible study with her in early August. It was scheduled to start the first of September. I know without a doubt that God had been working to prepare me for the trial that I was about to face. He is never surprised by anything, because He knows everything. He loves us enough to work behind the scenes and prepare us to face trials and tribulations in our lives.

In April when Troy had first said he was unhappy he made me promise not to share our problems with anyone. He said it was not anyone's business and we needed to keep it to ourselves. How wrong it was to make me promise that. I was dying inside, and I had no one to share my feelings with. Of course, in retrospect I realized if I had started talking to other people then someone would have found out what was really going on. I felt even more betrayed when I realized the real reason he made me promise that! He knew he was committing adultery and did not want anyone to find out. I beat myself up for a long time over that one, until I heard God's voice loud and clear. My ways are not your ways. I have a purpose and a plan. Trust Me, don't test Me.

As women, we are emotional by nature. We need to talk through our feelings. We need people close to us that we can trust to share our feelings with. God places godly women in our lives to speak to us, to comfort us, and to give us a support system. These sisters in Christ play a crucial role in our lives. It is critical to allow them to pray for us and build a wall of prayer around us.

The first person I called after I discovered the affair was a close cousin. She and her husband had been through the same thing years before and I apologized to her for not being there for her. I felt awful for not being able to understand the pain and heartache she went through at the time. We grew up almost like sisters and I knew I could always count on her, but I was not there for her during her time of need. Now,

I knew personally what it felt like to betrayed by the person you had given your life and your heart to. To know the person you loved had given his heart and body to someone other than you, lied and deceived you daily for months on end. My cousin's daily phone calls, love, support, and encouragement got me through some dark days. She had to talk me off the ledge several times. There will be some dark days and don't be surprised if you have some dark thoughts. There were days I wanted to disappear and thought everyone else would be better off without me. No matter how strong a Christian you are, these thoughts will come. It is crucial you have Godly women around you to help you in times of deep despair. Listen, and listen good! I understand! Your situation and mine may be different, but I get it! I am your friend and I want to help you through this. But more importantly, so does the Lord! He loves you! He knows your pain and He can help, just call on Him. I love the Lord and I could feel His love and strength infused inside of me. However, one thing I learned about myself through this process is that I am a very physical and emotional person. I need physical touch. As much as I love the Lord, He could not come down from Heaven and put his arms around me while I cried.

God provides for our needs in the most mysterious ways. My children suddenly became more loving and were constantly giving me hugs and snuggles. My parents and friends were always there to give me a big hug, even though they did not know what was going on. The solid Christian advice and support I received from my parents was overwhelming and I could feel their prayers making me stronger. I had several other close friends who were there for me as well and I don't know what I would have done without them. God has a defined purpose and reason for everything. This is difficult to believe when you are experiencing the harsh realities of your current situation. One of the things that really helped me were daily texts and emails from my mom. She would send me an encouraging scripture and song each day. Music can be a wonderful outlet for your emotions. It speaks to our soul and soothes us.

Who is your support system? If you do not have anyone, then ask God to send godly women into your life to help you. If you are not a

Christian, or do not have a personal relationship with Christ, there are other ways to find support as well. There are many online resources that will help you find infidelity support groups in your state. One such site is www.groups.psychologytoday.com. There are also online forums where you can post and talk with others in your unique situations such as www.SurvivingInfidelity.com. If you are not a member of a church but would like to have a Biblical perspective or support, do not hesitate to reach out to a local church in your area.

Gracie Kay

STEP THREE

Marriage or Christian Counseling

This was a hard step for me to take. My husband refused to seek help with me, but I knew I needed to see a professional with a Christian perspective to help me deal with this life-altering situation. It was less than a month after the discovery of the affair when I finally found someone I could meet with. I sat in a little soft chair in a bright sunroom of the ladies' home. I poured out my heart, only to have her look at me with this strange expression. "Oh dear, I am so sorry, but somewhere the wires got crossed. I only deal with children and families." If I hadn't been so shocked I probably would have laughed. She was sweet and apologetic, and I did feel a little better to have talked to someone. However, my peace was short lived.

I got a telephone call on my way back home from that visit. It seemed a certain someone's husband had found out; which I was told he had already been informed. Now, all of a sudden, I was to blame for him finding out. I sat in the parking lot of the closest store I could find. And proceeded to listen to how incompatible we were and how his heart was somewhere else. He said I could not stop him from leaving. I needed that counselor more than ever, but God has His own timeline. It took several weeks for me to see the right person (the one God knew I needed, but not the one I expected!). I did not feel comfortable talking with anyone in my church and I wanted someone who did not know my husband or myself. I needed someone to speak God's words of wisdom to me from a professional standpoint.

When I first started, I think I wanted her to tell me how God was going to fix everything. I needed her to assure me that everything was going to work out. That's not what happened. I'll never forget the first time I walked into her office. I was blessed with the bladder the size of a pea and it had been a long drive. After making a stop in the ladies' room, I walked into her office and said, "I can't wait to get to Heaven, so I can have a new bladder." She took one look at me, chuckled, and said, "Well, you are not at all what I expected." But, you see ladies, she wasn't what I expected either. Later we joked about it. She thought I would be much older and a complete and total train wreck after everything I had been through. I'm not really sure what I expected, but it was not a tiny and petite woman, not much older than me, but from a totally different race. But, our great and mighty God knew I would need her. We were sisters in Christ and that is what mattered! She helped me examine my life, my priorities, my behavior, but most importantly my relationship with the Lord. It is hard to learn things about yourself, but oh so rewarding to be able to learn and change and grow.

God created us with a variety of needs, such as physical, emotional, intellectual, psychological, and spiritual. According to *Philippians 4:19, "My God shall supply all your need according to His riches in glory by Christ Jesus." (KJV)* God is ready, willing, and able to meet all our needs. We find His help when we pray, study scriptures, listen to the Holy Spirit's leading, or from the counsel of godly and wise individuals. Sometimes these needs can be met through an individual whom God has directed us to. When going through life changing situations, it is important to seek counsel from wise and mature Christians (Proverbs 11:14). When our life needs are not met, we can experience mental anguish which in turn affects our daily activities and our relationships. When we find ourselves at this point, it is critical to seek counseling. Don't be embarrassed or ashamed to ask for help. The counselor, or therapist is there to provide healing, balance, and help you feel whole again. There are many methods which are used but make sure the sole focus is on the Lord as the Great Physician.

One of the most beneficial methods my therapist employed was helping me deal with my grief. While I did not physically lose a loved one, I was mourning the loss of my marriage and the brokenness that comes with adultery. The stages of grief as described by the Kubler-Ross model are as follows: Denial, Anger, Bargaining, and Depression.

During our bereavement, we spend different lengths of time working through each step and express each stage with different levels of intensity. Someone who is grieving may go through the stages in any order. We move between stages before achieving a more peaceful acceptance of our situation or loss.

<u>Denial</u> → "This can't be happening to me."
For me, the denial started many months prior to discovering the affair. It began when he first told me he wasn't happy. I think it was a subconscious denial along with the Lord keeping my eyes closed until the time was right for me to discover the affair. After discovering the affair though, the denial continued. I blamed the devil instead of understanding that my husband was the one who chose to willingly commit the sin of adultery.

<u>Anger</u> → "Why is this happening to me?"
My denial and anger went hand-in-hand. I was angry at first with the Lord for allowing this to happen to me. I certainly didn't feel like I deserved it and had always done everything I could to make my husband happy. But, being a Christian and living right doesn't shield you from rejection and hurt. I was also angry at my husband. After all I had given him, how could he do this to me? I quickly learned that anger leads to bitterness and causes separation from the Lord. Did I want the devil to win, or the Lord to have victory in my life? God forgives us so that we can forgive others. I realized then that I had to truly forgive my husband, the other woman, and myself.

<u>Bargaining</u> →"I will do anything to change this."
For months and months prior to discovering the truth, I constantly bargained with the Lord. I tried to "fix" myself and my marriage while begging Him to do something to open my husband's eyes.

<u>Depression</u> → "What's the point of going on after this loss?"
Immediately after discovering the affair, I was overwhelmed with many emotions. I fell into a deep depression. After

seeking medical help, starting therapy, and relying on my support group it lessened greatly. Staying in God's word and praying strategically and fervently helps. It allows my soul and my heart to have a modicum of happiness. Don't get me wrong, there are still moments and days that are dark, but in those times, I call on God's word, listen to uplifting music or simply "trust in the Lord."

Acceptance → "It's going to be okay."
I reached a breaking point several times in the past year. I remember one argument in particular when I stood up to my husband and made him talk to me. God helped me realize in that moment that I would be okay with or without my husband. I would survive. God was enough, and I was willing to sacrifice my love for my husband. I still pray daily, "even if he never truly loves me again, I pray he loves the Lord and becomes the man He wants him to be."

We all have different needs and the course of your therapy will depend upon your own personal needs. I attended therapy weekly for six weeks. I am very grateful to my therapist for helping me walk and talk through my feelings as well as offer spiritual guidance according to God's word. I would have loved to continue therapy, but finances were an issue as well as time off work. Any time you can invest into your personal mental and emotional well-being is invaluable time for you and your family. Remember, you must first take care of yourself, before you are able to take care of your family effectively.

☙ JOURNAL ❦

What actions do you feel you are taking to ensure you are caring for your well-being? Make a list of positive activities which you believe help you take care of yourself? These are different for each person. For example, it could be doing yoga, spending quiet time with your Bible or Devotional, taking a bubble bath every night, going to the gym routinely, taking vitamins or medications for your health, reading a book to help your mind escape, speaking to a counselor or therapist, or simply getting enough sleep each night.

STEP FOUR

Change Your Perspective and Hold onto Your Faith

My therapist suggested I find things that make me happy. For sixteen years, my life had been revolved around my husband, my kids, and my job. I never did anything for myself, and if I did, I felt guilty about being away from my kids. She helped me realize that I had to be the best me I could be, before being the best wife and mother God wanted me to be.

I stopped listening to Country music altogether because I couldn't stand to hear anything about love or heartbreak. I found Christian songs that uplifted and fed my soul. I even started going to the gym. This was very scary for me. I've never felt great about my body and I sure didn't want anyone to see me work out. But I got on the bicycle and took off so to speak. Well it was actually the elliptical machine and it didn't go anywhere physically. However, mentally it took me to wonderful places. Every time I stepped onto that machine and put in the ear buds the music would draw me into close communion and worship with the Lord. Not to mention I worked out a whole lot of frustration and got a great body in the process! I highly recommend making this time for yourself.

Writing has been the best therapy of all for me. There is something rewarding about putting your feelings on paper and setting them free to the Lord. When you talk about your feelings, there is a release, but when you write about them it helps you to gain perspective. When I would go back and read I found a new perspective. I had so many wonderful things in my life to be thankful for. I made lists of all the things that God had blessed me with and I posted them where I could see them. I have always been an optimistic person, but in the midst of the harsh reality of my current situation it was absolutely critical. If I didn't stay positive and strong I would fall apart again. It was crucial for me to learn that God doesn't work according to our time table. God's timing is not our timing. I know you hear that over and over again but let me say it one more time. God's timing is not our timing!

Engrave those words on your heart. Say them over until they become ingrained in your soul. Naturally you will be angry with your spouse and even the Lord. You will question "Why?" and wonder what you did wrong. But I encourage you to find one positive thing in your life and hold onto it. For me it was my oldest son's story.

In the weeks and months that followed I realized he had carried a tremendous burden. He came to me one day when I was crying and told me he was sorry. I looked at him with this strange look on my face. "I knew mama. I knew he was talking to her and texting her. It didn't feel right, and I didn't know what to do. I should have told you and I am sorry." He had seen who his daddy had been texting and put two and two together, so to speak. Talk about a mad mamma bear! Well that was me! I was mad at my husband for unwittingly putting our child in this position. However, I did not let my son see this reaction. I held him close and told him it was not his fault and he had done nothing wrong. I explained to him that God has His own time frame and purpose and that none of this was his fault.

But, there's a silver lining in this cloud. In the late Summer, my son had the opportunity to attend Church camp with some friends. While there he was in a small group Bible Study with a young man that he quickly became friends with. He said he felt the Lord speaking to him through the scriptures, the music and the words of his new friends. He realized he was missing something in his life. He had a heavy burden because he was carrying part of his dad's sin, but he also recognized he carried sin in his heart as well. He asked the Lord to forgive him of his sins and to come into his heart and save him. He was gloriously saved at church camp! Every time I find myself sinking back into that black abyss of depression or want to wallow in the past I remember my son's salvation and the health of my three beautiful children that God had blessed me with. I do not know if the affair had to happen, in order for my child to get saved. However, I do realize that God can use anything that happens and turn it into something for His glory. I was reminded of Genesis 50:20, which says, *"As for you, ye thought evil against me, but God meant it unto good, to bring to pass, as it is this day, to save much people alive." (KJV)* Remember, God always has a purpose and a plan. Sometimes we will discover the purpose, and sometimes we do not. For my faith, it is important to remember, everything in my life that happens is not a random chain of events, but it is all according to God's plan, not my own. I spent all those months praying for God to open my husband's eyes, but I never prayed for His Will to be done. The song, "Thy will be done," by Hillary Scott and Family describes my feelings. I encourage you to listen to this song and remember we serve a mighty God. There will be many times in your life when you are confused, blindsided, or just dumbfounded by events you are faced with. Sometimes we think we hear God's voice loud and clear, but we end up going down a path we never thought we'd be on. When we find ourselves in this place in our lives, fall on our knees in prayer and simply pray for God's will to be done. In this moment of submission, He will help you change your perspective and guide you on your journey.

ೞ **JOURNAL** ೞ

How can you change your perspective? Take a few moments and write a prayer or just a few thoughts that can help you in this area. Try to list one thing you can hold on to.

_____

_____

_____

_____

_____

_____

_____

_____

STEP FIVE

The Making

In the beginning, I was broken and hollow. God allowed this circumstance to come into my life to mold me and make me into a God-strengthened woman of faith who could be of service to him. When I reached step five the Lord was beginning the process of making and refining me.

When I was a young preteen I was fascinated with pottery and clay. I remember for my ninth or tenth birthday I received a pottery wheel. I was ecstatic! I would take my lump of clay and place it on my wheel. Then I would dip my hands in water, place my hands around the lump, and turn the wheel on. I would have to keep constant pressure on the clay and constantly mold it as it turned on the wheel. Round and around it would go. When the process was over I had a beautiful bowl or cup of art. But I didn't stop there. The product was not finished. If left to dry it would crack and fall apart and not be stable or useful for anything. I had to kill it in a kiln. I had to try it by fire before it could be made perfect!

Of course, as a young girl I did not see the symbolism behind the pottery I was creating. At the time it was simply fun to create art with my hands. The other day I came across a piece that one of my kids had made for me in Art class. I've had it for seven years and it is still beautiful and in perfect condition. It struck me in that moment: I am God's work of art. According to Psalm 139:14, I am "fearfully and wonderfully made," and the Lord does not make any mistakes.

One of my favorite men in the Bible is the prophet Jeremiah. God set before him one difficult task after another and he experienced deep emotional conflict. He was honest and true with God, often 'weeping' over what he was asked to do. There were many things he did not understand, but he trusted God anyway and stayed true to God's calling throughout it all. There are many glimpses of hope throughout the book of Jeremiah. I love Chapter 18:6, which says, *"Like clay is hand of the potter, so are you in my hand, Israel." (NIV)* Now I know he was talking to the nation of Israel here, but it is such a comfort to know that I am clay in God's hand. He will mold me, make, and perfect me into something beautiful and useful. We are clay in the hands of the great and mighty God!

> Thou art the potter, I am the clay, mold me and make me after thy will, while I am waiting yielded and still.

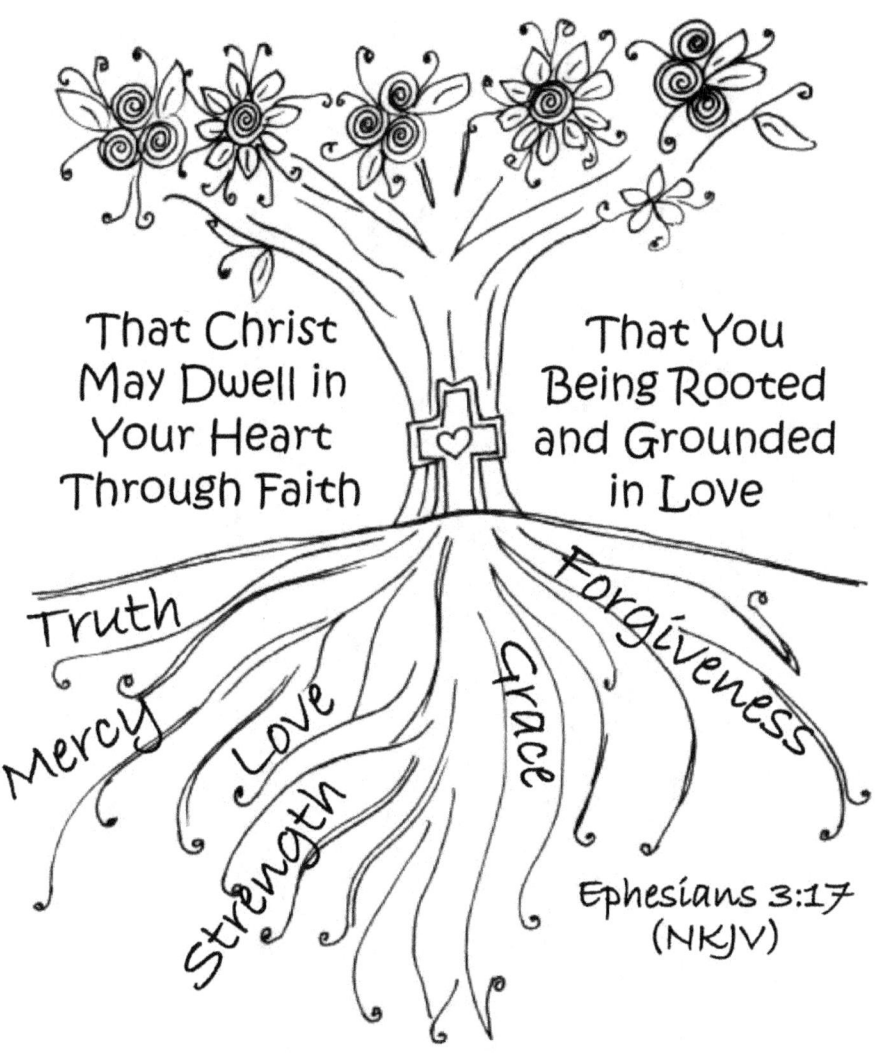

Gracie Kay

Draw Close to the Lord and Live Loved!

The oxygen we breathe fills our lungs and helps us survive, but what helps our soul survive? If you have asked the Lord to come into your heart and save you from your sins, then He becomes the oxygen for your soul. His love fills me. If I am loved by God I am no longer empty. "Being full of God's love settles, empowers, and brings out the best of who we are."

In Ephesians 3:14-19, Paul shares a prayer with believers:

For this reason, I kneel before the Father, from whom every family in heaven and on earth derives its name. I pray that out of his glorious riches he may strengthen you with power through his Spirit in your inner being, so that Christ may dwell in your hearts through faith. And I pray that you, being rooted and established in love, may have power, together With all the Lord's holy people, to grasp how wide and long and high and deep is the love of Christ, and to know this love that surpasses knowledge-that you may be filled to the measure of all the fullness of God. (NIV)

Paul shares some great promises from God with us. God is the creator of all, but only those who have a personal relationship with Him may call him Father. God's resources are limitless, and He grants us an inner strength in our present experiences or circumstances. When we allow Him to empower us, He has access to every area of our lives. If we allow Him, His love will give us a peace that we never imagined, empower us with strength to face things we can never survive on our own, and mold us into the godly women we are all capable of becoming.

All humans crave acceptance and fulfillment that comes from being loved. During this trial God began to reveal many things to me through prayer and His word. Let me warn you though, don't expect the Lord to change your husband without changing you in the process. Yes, I said it "change." None of us are perfect and we all have room for change. I realized I had been looking to my husband for love and acceptance. In a way, I was putting him before God. I was so ashamed when He revealed this to me. I wasn't living loved because I was looking to my husband to complete me. As a result, I was constantly disappointed. The expectations I had were unrealistic and could not possibly be met. I had to lay down all my expectations to the Lord and get out of the way, so He could get in the way!

But if I grasp the full love of Christ, if I soak His words into my soul and allow Him to shower me with His love, then I won't grab at other people or other things to fill me. A light went on in my soul and a peace came over me. I no longer had to live in fear of my husband's rejection because God's love was able to fill me and give me a strength that I could never possess on my own. The more time I spent with God, the more time I spent in His word, and the more I invited His love to fill me, the less I felt uninvited, unloved, and unworthy by others!

ಎ JOURNAL ೞ

How do you feel about God's love? What fulfills you and makes you feel His love? In your own words describe how God loves you.

_____

_____

_____

_____

_____

_____

_____

_____

_____

_____

_____

# THE BREAKING AND MAKING OF ME

Gracie Kay

STEP SIX

Declaring War with The Real Enemy and Preparing Your War Room

When the movie 'War Room' was available on video, our church had a movie night and we all piled up together with our popcorn and drinks and watched it on a screen in the basement. Of course, my husband wasn't there to see it. I remember watching, crying and being inspired by Priscilla Shrirer; the main actress. It was such a wonderful movie. The movie is about the Jordan family, who seems to have it all: wealth, success and a beautiful daughter. However, the husband becomes entangled with sin and fights with temptation, while the wife becomes increasingly bitter and does not know what to do about her failing marriage. Then the wife meets her new client, an older woman shows her how to fight the devil and regain happiness. How could I have known this movie would be a foreshadowing of my life just a few short months later. He was seeing her at the time and I was unaware of it, but God knew, and He was preparing me for the trial to come.

Rejection isn't just an emotion we feel. It's a message engraved into our hearts and our souls. It causes us to believe lies about ourselves, other people and God himself. Being spiritually mature does not shield us from rejection either. Rejection causes us to question everything we think about our identity. Our world comes crashing down around us and we can no longer see goodness in our lives.

But in the face of this ultimate rejection we must be so very careful to *"guard our hearts and minds through Christ Jesus." (Philippians 4:7 NIV).*

You see ladies, the devil is right there waiting in the dark shadows. He's the real enemy. It's not your spouse, and not even the other woman. It's normal to feel anger, hurt, pain, disbelief, and rejection. But, we must be careful not to let these emotions control us or the devil will use them against us. His sole purpose is to *"steal, kill, and destroy." John 10:10 (NIV).* In 1 Peter 5:8, the Lord tells us to, *"be sober, be vigilant; because your adversary the devil, as a roaring lion, walketh about, seeking whom he may devour." (KJV)* If he destroys the marriage, he destroys the family. Remember this is the devil's ultimate goal.

Stop for just a moment and think. Do you want the devil to win? He is vicious, and he may win for a season of our lives, but he will not be victorious. Unless of course we let him.

There came a very dark night about a month after I found out about the affair when I had to make a choice. That night my husband chose not to come home and I knew where he was. What I thought was a short-lived affair was not over. I realized the devil still had a very stronghold on my husband and he was using this other person to confuse, manipulate and control him. I knew right then and there this was going to be the fight of my life. This was war and my enemy, the devil, was alive and well! But in order to be prepared for this battle, I had to reexamine everything I thought I knew, not just about myself as a Christian, but the Lord as well. I had to rediscover the "truth" of who God is and His nature.

God is Good! He is good all the time. His plans are good. His salvation and grace are good. Even though I was in the midst of this terrible circumstance, this was not by God's design. I want you to hear me loud and clear---God did not cause this to happen to you! Sin did! Sin had caused my marriage and my heart to be broken into pieces. I knew God was good and God was good to me. There's a line from one of my favorite songs entitled 'Tell Your Heart to Beat Again' by Danny Gokey, where the artist talks about while we are going through trials in that moment God is working behind the scenes working everything for our good. In order to experience true joy, then I had to truly trust God to be God.

So, once I understood God's nature and truly learned to trust him I realized that He has all the tools I needed for battle. The ladies at my church had been planning to do a bible study with the book 'Fervent' by Priscilla Shrirer. This book inspired the movie 'War Room'. I had the book in my possession for months because the Bible study never started. That night, God spoke to me and told me it was time to read it because the answers I needed could be found in the pages of the book. Prayer would become my most powerful weapon of all.

I marched into my bedroom like a crazed woman on a mission. Swinging open the door to my walk-in closet I moved clothes until I had a blank wall; a blank canvas for my prayers; my own war room! Standing in the middle of my bedroom I yelled out to the devil, "From this day forward, you no longer have control over this family. You are not welcome in this home or in the lives of my family. My family belongs to Christ and you will leave us alone. Bring it on devil! I am no longer going to sit idly by and watch you destroy my husband, my marriage, my family, and my home. My God is all powerful and He has already won this war."

I know this may seem a little drastic to some of you and even a little crazy. But the devil is real, and he does have power. In Ephesians 6:12, the Lord makes this very clear:

For we wrestle not against flesh and blood, but against principalities, against powers, against the rulers of the darkness of this world, against spiritual wickedness in high places. (KJV)

The devil had been creeping into my mind and constantly reminding me of the hurt and pain.

The mind feasts on what it focuses on. What consumes my thinking Will be the making or breaking of my identity.
Uninvited by Lysa TerKeurst

Is this what any of you want? It certainly wasn't what I wanted. I could no longer allow the devil to have control over my mind and to feast on the pain, the hurt, or the rejection. I was obsessed with the past. I was focused on reliving every detail of our lives from the past seven months. What was real? What was not? There was no memory from that time period that I felt was real, except the memories I made with my children that did not include my husband. But no matter how hard we wish and hope, we cannot go back. The past is in the past. We cannot change it. It happened, and we can only move forward. I had to trust God to the point where I was willing to turn over full control of my life, my husband's life, and my family to Him alone!

൭ **JOURNAL** ൫

Take a moment and write down some of your favorite scriptures that help encourage you or make you feel the power and love of Christ!

_____

_____

_____

_____

_____

_____

_____

_____

_____

_____

_____

_____

_____

_____

_____

_____

_____

THE BREAKING AND MAKING OF ME

Gracie Kay

Gracie Kay

STEP SEVEN

Strategic Prayer

I never knew my prayer life was not effective. I spent months praying for God to change my husband and open his eyes, but my heart was not in the right place. I was praying in anger and wanting God to give my husband what he deserved. My heart and my motives were not pure and right in God's eyes. I also was not being strategic. I was merely praying blanket prayers and not identifying specific ways the devil was targeting my family.

How do you change the way you pray? In the book 'Fervent', Priscilla Shirer reveals how to formulate a battle plan through strategic, specific, and fervent prayer. The devil targets so many things in our lives that we do not even realize. I have been a Christian for most of my life and I am ashamed to tell you I did not realize how much power the devil has in our lives. You will never know how truly real the devil is until he comes after your family. Mrs. Shrirer talks about ten different areas the devil attacks.

I read the book and applied all prayer strategies to my prayer life. However, the longer I prayed and drew near to the Lord, the more I learned about how to pray. He began to share with me different strategies that were specific to my situation. I want to share with you these strategies and what the Lord revealed to me.

A Prayer for My Identity
Who Am I Lord?

In the aftermath of adultery, let me assure you that you will face a major identity crisis. You will question who you are, what your life is worth, and what kind of person you are. I remember questioning my husband, "What does she have that I don't have? What is wrong with my body? What do you like about me? What is something nice you can say about me?" I remember staring in the mirror trying to figure out who I was.

Don't despair. It is only natural to go through this. It doesn't make you any less of a woman. You will never know who you truly are until you know who God really is. Remember you are loved by God! You are a treasured daughter of the Lord and He will strengthen you and uphold you. Look to the scripture and lay claim to your identity in Christ. Discover all the wonderful things God has done for you.

Who Am I In Christ?

*I am chosen by God	Ephesians 1:4
I am adopted by God	Ephesians 1:5
I am sealed with God's Holy Spirit	Ephesians 1:13
I am redeemed-bought with Christ's blood	Ephesians 1:7
I am a full citizen among God's people	Ephesians 2:19
I am cleansed by Christ's blood for all my sins!	I John 1:7
I am a child of God in His family	I John 3:1
I am forgiven by God for all my sins	I John 1:9
I am justified-declared right in God's sight	Romans 5:1
I am reconciled to God, in harmony with Him	Romans 5:10
I am heir of God and a joint-heir with Christ	Romans 8:16,17
I am being conformed to the character of Chris	Romans 8:29
*I am called to accomplish God's purpose	Romans 8:28,30
*I am complete in Christ	Colossians 2:10
*I am seen by God as holy, blameless, and above reproach	Colossians 1:21,22

| I am sanctified-set apart by God's spirit | I Corinthians 6:11 |
| I am an ambassador for Christ | 2 Corinthians 5:20 |

Every time I feel my identity wavering, I look to these scriptures to help remind me of who I am in Christ. They are all very powerful and true, but the ones I starred are very close to my heart! I am chosen by God. He chose to create me. He chose to invite me into His family. He chose to die for my sins. He chose to love me. He chose me, and I matter.

> *"And we know that all things work together for good to those who are the called according to His purpose. For whom He foreknew, He also predestined to be conformed to the image of His Son, that He might be the firstborn among many brethren. Moreover, whom He predestined, these He also called, whom He called, these He also justified, and whom He justified He also glorified." Romans 8:28-30 (NKJV)*

There are many great promises in these verses. God promises to overrule and work even through tragedies in our lives caused by sin's presence in the world. He promises to accomplish His purposes in the lives of those who love Him and have responded to His call. As a Christian woman who belongs to the Lord, I know that no matter how bad it gets, His work, His will, and His ways will be accomplished.

I am being conformed to the character of Christ and I am called to accomplish God's purpose. I am complete in Christ. Talk about life changing words! My husband could never complete me because he is human, and I placed unreal expectations on him. I created this ideal man that I deserved and was constantly rejected every time he failed to live up to my standards. Of course, I didn't realize I was doing any of this until God revealed it unto me. You see our God is a jealous God. He wants us to love Him with our whole heart. Once this was revealed, I knew God was everything I needed. He gives me worth, meaning, and shows me I have a purpose. For years, I believed my purpose was to be a good wife, a good mother, and to excel in the career which God had given me. Now, I feel as though the Lord might be showing me a different purpose for my life; to help other women and to minister through my writing.

Don't let the heartbreak or rejection destroy your identity. Let the breaking be the making of a newer and stronger you. Allow God to use it to make you a refined and stronger Godly woman. (Psalms 34:18). Remember the Lord is always right there offering you His grace and strength! Call on the Lord's strength through prayer. We can do this specifically and strategically when we articulate our needs, our wants, our desires, or simply worship and praise the Lord. Read the following prayer from my heart and allow God to empower you as well.

Dear Lord,

I know the devil wants me to feel weak, worthless, unloved, set aside and confused! But I am one of your treasured daughters. I am loved by you completely! I am chosen by you. I am set apart for a purpose. Help me to be constantly filled with your grace, your joy and your Holy Spirit! I know with you Lord I am empowered, and I am beautiful!

Gracie Kay

A Prayer for Passion and Purpose
Where Is My Passion? What Is My Purpose?

Looking back and examining our lives, I see that the devil had attacked and stolen our passion for the Lord. Of course, we were faithful to the house of the Lord and God does reward faithfulness. However, we had lost the passion for serving. Our busy lives had taken place of our close relationship with the Lord. If you played sports as a young person, then you know the intensity with which you practiced, maybe the passion which you displayed drove you to be a better player. If we serve God with the same intensity and passion imagine what we can accomplish.

Passion
- o An intense desire or enthusiasm for something.
- o A thing arousing enthusiasm.

I always imagined my purpose in life was to be a Godly wife, mother, and teacher. If I did all three of those to the best of my ability, then surely, I was fulfilling God's purpose for my life. But what if God desires much more for me and for you? What if He has a greater purpose in mind for us than we could ever imagine? I love the definition I came across for purpose:

Purpose
- o The reason for which something is done or created or for which something exists.
- o A person's sense of resolve or determination. have as one's intention or objective.

This definition is three-fold. What possible reason could the Lord have for allowing adultery to enter into my marriage? What possible reason could the Lord have for creating such a horrible situation to happen in my life? What is the reason I exist? It is only natural to wonder about your purpose during trying times. However, it is extremely important to remember that God did not willingly allow your spouse or my spouse to commit adultery. God always provides a way out of any tempting situation, but it is up to the will of that person to ask for a way out. Talk about an eye opener when the Lord revealed this to me! In 1 Corinthians 10:13, it says,

"No temptation has overtaken you except such as is common to man; but God is faithful, who will not allow you to be tempted beyond what you are able, but with the temptation will also make the way of escape, that you may be able to bear it." (NKJV)

He gives man free will. It is our sins and desires that draw us away from God and causes us to fall into sin. We all have a choice. One afternoon in November, I was sitting on the floor crying and trying to get my husband to talk to me. I remember asking him why he did not choose a way out? He willingly chose to commit adultery and to break our marriage covenant. He had a choice, but he made the wrong one. God has a purpose for the pain and the trial. He has a purpose for all of our pain as we travel down this road together. When the time is right He will reveal it unto us. God will also reveal through the trial a greater purpose for your life and your husbands. I am ashamed to say that I never even gave a thought to my husband's purpose. But, you can bet your bottom dollar it is constantly on my mind now! I can't put pressure on my husband to be something, but I can pray for him to become something. I can pray for us both to be molded according to God's plan, and not anyone else's.

Dear Lord,

I pray that you will restore passion unto my husband and myself. May we both crave and desire a more intimate relationship with You. I pray that you would reveal your purpose unto both of us. I desire a passionate and close relationship with You. Help me to maintain this passion in every area of my life. Help me to maintain my passion for fervent and specific prayer. I trust Your Word and Your promises. I expect to see miracles from You!

A Prayer for My Family

Did you know you have some control over your children and your husband's future? No, we cannot play God, but through specific and strategic prayer, we can accomplish mighty things. Satan wants to destroy, tempt, and break your family unit to pieces. However, we can intercede for our family and keep the devil from gaining anymore ground. One night in particular, I was fed up with the devil and decided to take my house back! I went to every room in my house and prayed for the devil's presence and control to be removed. I took back my house and proclaimed that Satan could go back to where he belonged. (Luckily no one was home, or my children would surely have thought their mama had lost her mind!)

Let's think about the word 'Family' for a moment. When praying, I like to think about each of these areas of my loved one's lives.

> F→ Their Future and Their Faith
>
> A→ Attitude

M→   Matters of The Heart

I→   Independence

L→   Live Loved

Y→   You (Being Who God Wants Them to Be)

F→ Praying for your children and your spouse's future and their faith is extremely important. The world in which we live is growing increasingly wicked and our loved ones will need a strong faith in God in order to survive and stay strong in Christ. We can pray that God guides them down the right paths and their future is secured in Him alone.

A→ I am often complemented on the manners my children have which I am very thankful for. However, I want my children to have more than terrific manners. I want my husband and my children to have a Godly attitude. I want others to see His light in them.

M→ We must also pray about the matters of the heart. The heart is deceitfully wicked; who can know it? We all tell our children to follow their hearts, but what if their heart is telling them to do something contrary to God's word? We must pray that our children and our spouse's steps always be in sync with His Will. The devil can very easily sneak in and turn our heart against us.

I→ If our children and our spouse our living the right way, then they will lead independent and God filled lives. We want them to be strong and self-sufficient children of God. Pray they will find and know their inner strength and independence.

L→ In this day and age with so much wickedness in the world, so many pressures, and every day stress in our lives and the lives of our family, it is difficult to not feel constantly overwhelmed.

Always pray for your family to know and to feel God's love personally. Pray they will live a life filled with His LOVE!

Y→ Always pray for your children and your spouse to be the "you" God wants them to be and that their hearts and minds are fixed on His direction and will for their lives. It can be very easy to succumb to peer pressures as children and as an adult. If we are not careful, we will find ourselves wanting to dress and act like others and even covet what they have. God wants us to be content with what He has given us. Pray for your family to know who they are in Christ and to be thankful for his blessings!

Dear Lord,

You have given me a wonderful family. You have blessed me with a husband and three beautiful children. I pray that I will be a godly wife to my husband and a godly mother to my children. I pray for their future, their faith, their attitudes, their heart, and their independence. I pray they will live life loved and full of Your grace and mercy. But most of all Lord, I pray that they would be who You want them to be and always follow Your will for their lives!

A Prayer for My Past and My Hurts

This has been perhaps one of the most difficult prayer strategies to implement. It is still a struggle to overcome the past and the deep hurts that scar you for life. When I first started down this path, I thought I would have no problem forgiving and forgetting. But I can honestly say it is a daily battle. Yes, time heals wounds, but some things can never be truly forgotten. During a New Year's sermon, my pastor talked about how we must look to the past in order to face the future. It hit so close to home for me. In order to move forward, you must first go back. There is so much you can learn about the future by looking at the past.

However, what we must remember, what we must not forget, is the lesson that God wants us to learn. He does not want us to dwell on the past, but to learn from it and to be set free from it! God doesn't live in the past and we only live by grace anyway. Once we ask for forgiveness He completely forgets the past, so why can't we?

Satan on the other hand wants us to be enslaved to the past. He wants us to feel constant shame, guilt, and regret. The devil wants us to have an unforgiving heart to cause bitterness and separation from God. He wants us to constantly be reminded of past hurts and pain. If we are constantly dwelling on the past, our hurts, our failures, our sins, our mistakes, then he is winning and not the Lord! Remember we are fighting a battle. Satan may be victorious for a season, but God has already won the war!

We must strive to forget and forgive. I know we have all heard this since childhood, but I have lived it. Not only must we strive to put the past behind us, we must forgive those who have wronged us as well. In Matthew 6:14 and 15, God makes this very clear. *"For if you forgive men their trespasses, your heavenly Father will also forgive you. But if you do not forgive men their trespasses, neither will your Father forgive your trespasses."* (NKJV) God forgives all our sins, so why can't we forgive those who have wronged us? It was extremely difficult to forgive my husband and the other woman, and it has taken a very long time, but once I did a peace settled over me. Forgiveness really does set you free!

Dear Lord,

I know that Satan wants me to feel constant shame, guilt and regret about the past. HE wants me to constantly dwell on the hurt and pain and cause my heart to become hard and bitter. Help me to remember that prayer can change even unchangeable things! Lord, you forgive us, so it is possible to forgive others. Forgiveness makes us free! Help me to have a spirit of forgiveness. Help my spouse to have a spirit of forgiveness.

A Prayer for My Fears

Imagine a four-year old girl bounding ahead of her family in a hurry to get to her toys. She is almost to the top of the stairs when she sees a light on. She pauses for a second when she hears heavy breathing. Then she sees a flash of black as a man runs past her. She screams, her joy, now fear, and her dad comes running. Her joy turned to fear in an instant!

That young girl was me. I had the misfortune to walk in on a burglar at a very young age. Fear of the dark came quickly after that event in my life. If remained for years. The fear brought nightmares. All of this continued until about the age of ten. Then my parents decided I was old enough to talk with my pastor about my fears. I remember talking and crying to him. He gave me a big bear hug and told me how much God loved me and didn't want me to be afraid. He then showed me some scriptures. I don't remember the scriptures (motherhood removes a few brain cells). However, I will never forget what he said: "Fear is just false evidence appearing to be real. The devil is playing tricks on your mind.'

Let's look at this for just a moment:

False
Evidence
Appearing to be
Real

Throughout my childhood and adult life this has stuck with me. I never imagined at this point in my life it would become almost a mantra for me. Adultery brings along with it is so many fears. Some are real and warranted, while others are not. The devil wants to use our fears against us. He wants to paralyze us in that moment in time and keep us from moving forward. If he controls our mind, he controls us. If he controls us, then God can't move in us! He wants to cripple us and keep us from our destinies. Remember, our minds feasts on what it focuses on. We must lean on God's strength and trust in His promises. God already knows our heart and our thoughts, so be honest with him. Make a list and shout them out to Him. Pray through them!

As a child, I had horrible nightmares and they returned full force during the months after the adultery. You see, when I was wide awake the Lord had complete control of my thoughts. I stayed saturated in His word and kept all my thoughts on things above. The only chance the devil had to get into my mind was through my subconscious thoughts at night. And let me tell you, they were not pretty! They were so real, and the FEAR was so horrible! Of course, I could play the psych card and interpret all of them for you, but it still didn't stop them from coming.

Then one night, during a really bad nightmare I started screaming, "I am not afraid!" I remember repeating this over and over again. I awoke myself and my husband screaming those words. When I was wide awake a calm came over me. The nightmares didn't leave right away, but slowly turned to bad dreams, then just dreams. The devil no longer had control over my thoughts! I like to think of an acapella song two ladies I know sing. Their words talk about God's power sustaining us in the shadows and the storm. We will always be safe because God's arms are holding us!

Dear Lord,

Help me to remember that Satan wants me to be afraid! He wants to intimidate me and paralyze me with fear! He wants me to focus on my fears, so I lose focus on You! Help me to remember You have not given me a "spirit of fear, but of power, of might, and a sound mind." If Satan is working on my fear, then I know there is a blessing or a beauty from heaven waiting for me
just ahead!

A Prayer for My Heart and My Love
As a young girl, I remember following my heart many times. How could I go wrong if I "listened to my heart"? It took my husband's infidelity for me to realize that *"the heart is deceitful above all things, and desperately wicked; Who can know it?" Jeremiah 17:9 (NJKV)*

It's not wrong to follow your heart, but we must be oh so careful and make sure we have a clean and pure heart first. *"Create in me a clean heart, O God, and renew a right spirit within me." Psalms 51:10 (NJKV)*

Proverbs 3:5-6 tells us in whom to place our trust. *"Trust in the Lord with all thine heart and lean not unto thine own understanding. In all thy ways acknowledge him, and he shall direct your paths." (KJV)* I love this promise from the Lord! The Hebrew word for direct is "yashar", which literally means to make smooth, straight or right! We must trust Him with our all, with every part of our life. We must lean on Him completely and acknowledge Him.

To acknowledge literally means to accept or admit the existence of truth. God is the truth and His ways are to be trusted! If we do these things, then He will smooth out our path and remove obstacles in our way. He doesn't say when or how, He just promises that He will.

I realized early on that the Lord was teaching me how to show unconditional love to my husband. The Lord loves us with no strings attached, no matter how much we mess up or how little we love Him in return. This is one of the many lessons He wanted me to learn. I must be patient to preserve and wait for God to redeem, to restore, and to revive that which has been lost! There have been many days where I have felt like giving up and believe me you will face many as well. After multiple separations, broken promises and lots of tears there were many times I felt like giving up. Every time, God would show me something to restore my hope. Sometimes it was a Bible verse. Sometimes it was a song on the radio that spoke to my heart. Other times it was a phone call or a text from a friend. God restored my hope each and every time. Did my husband deserve for me to be so patient and longsuffering? No! BUT, then again none of us deserve the patience and grace God extends to us every day! God has promised,

"My grace is sufficient for thee: for my strength is made perfect in weakness. Most gladly therefore will I rather glory in my infirmities, that the power of Christ may rest upon me." 2 Corinthians 12:9 (KJV)

Dear Lord,

I pray that you will continue to create in me a clean and pure heart every day. Fill me with Your love and desires. I want to follow my heart, but only if my heart first belongs to You! Forgive me for putting my spouse and my children before You. I give you all my heart. I love You with all my heart, my soul and my might. I believe You will direct my path, my heart, my love, and my journey. Help me to fully trust You each and every day! Be my guide all the way!

Gracie Kay

A Prayer for My Focus and Perspective

Resolve to keep happy and your joy and you shall form an invincible host against difficulties.
- Helen Keller

When a photographer brings the camera lens into focus, the image he wants to capture becomes clear. In life when we stay centered on the Lord our focus helps us accomplish many things. Focus helps minimize distractions. It helps keep us from being blindsided like I was all those months ago. It helps us not to become preoccupied or overlook important details because we are paying close attention to the word of the Lord. It keeps our goals and dreams from being consumed or sidelined by the devil's plans. He wants to enslave us with so much pressure, stress and chaos in our everyday lives. He wants us to not feel satisfied with who or what we have.

Focus helps us to see the real enemy and his game plan! It is Satan and it always has been! His greatest game plan is to destroy families! He wants to control and manipulate us, so we can't see his crafty ways.

For we wrestle not against flesh and blood, but against principalities, against powers, against the rulers of darkness of this world, against spiritual wickedness in high places.
Ephesians 6:12 (KJV)

My faith, my focus, and my perspective were all tested in December 2017. Two weeks before Christmas, we ended up in the emergency room with one of our children. Our child had a severe infection and he was fighting for his life. We were by his side day and night. During this time, my husband received a text message from the other woman and I just happened to intercept it. Our child was dying and it seemed she was still in the picture. Satan was doing his best to destroy all my hope and faith. But, we received a miracle that Christmas and our son was healed. God used that event to help me become even more focused and fight harder for our family.

Satan is the real enemy. He wants me to lose my focus, my self-control, and my temper. In prayer, I am joining my weak spirit with God's Holy Spirit and all the power of heaven to fight Satan directly.

Dear Lord,

Please help me to keep my focus on You at all times. Help me to remember that Satan is the real enemy, not my spouse, not our finances, not the situation. He is the author of confusion. He is behind all the arguments, strife and troubles we are facing. He has a strategy and a game plan and that is to destroy my family! You have not given me "a spirit of fear, but of power, of might, and a sound mind." When I pray I am joining my weak spirit with your Holy Spirit. You give me power to fight Satan directly!

A Prayer for My Husband

In reality, this should have been my first strategy to implement but to be honest I had to get to the point where my heart was right, and where I could pray for him with a heart filled with unconditional love. Since that time, I have made it a habit to pray for every aspect of my husband's life. I am ashamed that I never realized how important it was to pray for my spouse. Praying for your husband is not about making him pay for what he has done. We must have a heart that longs to do right more than be right! We must have a desire to give life more than get even! Prayer is God's greatest tool of restoration. One day when I was praying it struck me just how much power God gives unto those who pray with a selfless heart. He gives us *"authority... over all power of the enemy." Luke 10:19 (NKJV).* Want to make a dent in the devil's plans? Then pray like your life and those you loved depends on it. We must submit to God in prayer whatever controls your husband

and your marriage- infidelity, alcoholism, workaholism, depression, anxiety, or fear. We must truly trust God to take care of these problems. In Stormie O'Martian's book 'The Power of a Praying Wife', she talks about thirty specific prayers we should pray for our spouse. I keep her book beside my Bible in my prayer closet and refer to it each day. Some of the most important areas for me to pray for in my husband's life are: his past, his attitude, his trials, his marriage, his temptations, his affection, his choices, his repentance, his deliverance, his obedience, and his future.

I know what it feels like to long for your spouse to look into your soul and see who you really are, to live with and love with someone who doesn't love you with their whole heart. But, how many times has God loved us when we are yet un-loveable? We must show our husband the same unconditional love every day. When we do that, God will take away the pain, hopelessness, the hurt, the hardness, and the unforgiving spirit we have towards our husband. There is amazing joy in seeing something hopelessly dead brought back to life. The very power that resurrected our Lord and Savior from the grave is the very same power that can resurrect the deadness in our marriage! Think about that one for a while! He can, and He will redeem, restore, and revive that which has been lost. We have to go through the pain to get to the joy, but God's way is the only way to save your marriage! Be patient. It may happen quickly, or it may take a long time. It depends on the lessons He wants you and your spouse to learn along the way. Some men and women have a harder head than others. There may be days you feel like you are the one being punished. I have been there. Nine months after the initial discovery, I received an even greater blow. I was given information that confirmed my suspicion that he was still seeing her. Every promise he made me was broken. More lies and more deception. I was forced to ask him to leave. All those months I was the only one who had been trying. She still had power over him. I did not understand why he could not give it over to the Lord and let Him take control. The night I asked him to leave there was no emotion in his eyes. I realized in that moment there was nothing I could do or say. He was lost and confused and there was nothing I could do but pray. It's our job to pray and God's job to answer. How and when He does is all according to His plan and purpose.

Dear Lord,

Help me to lay down my life in prayer for my husband every day. Help me to love him with the same unconditional love that You love us with! Use me as an instrument in his deliverance Lord. May he find peace, joy and comfort in our home and in our marriage. May we both view our marriage not the way it was, or the way it is, but the way You want it to be. May You give us both a clear vision for the future and unify us with Your love. Make my heart right and show me how to be a Godly wife. Give me a new husband by making him a new creation in You Lord. Show me specific areas of his life that I should be praying for. Nothing is too far gone that you cannot resurrect; You can save my marriage! Help me to remember as long as I am praying, there is hope!

Gracie Kay

Gracie Kay

STEP EIGHT

Trusting in God's Truths and Promises

"The truth shall set make you free." John 8:32 *(KJV)* We've all heard this famous quote from the Bible, but what does it really mean? The truths I have learned about who God is, how much He loves me, and His many promises have been life changing! God's love and His goodness we all can count on. His love and goodness will always be there and will always follow us! I wrote the following words and posted them on the wall in my war room.

> *Lord You are teaching me so much about trusting You.*
> *Fully. Completely. Without suggestions or projections.*
> *I'm choosing to embrace the very next thing*
> *You show me. I'll take the first step. And then I'll take the next.*
> *I finally understand I don't have to fully understand*
> *each thing that happens for me to trust You.*
> *I don't have to try and figure it out, control it, or even like it, for that matter.*
> *In the midst of uncertainties, I will just stand and say, "I trust You Lord."*

This prayer comes straight from Lysa TerKeurst's book 'Uninvited'. With this trust, with this truth my soul felt absolutely free. The following days, weeks, and months would be hard. Don't fool yourself because there will be many dark days ahead. But praying, trusting and living loved by my Heavenly Father, I knew I was prepared to face what laid ahead.

My life verses are Philippians 4:11-13:

> *Not that I speak in respect of want:*
> *For I have learned in whatsoever state I am, therewith to be content.*
> *I know both how to be abased, and I know how to abound:*
> *everywhere and in all things I am instructed to be full and to be hungry,*
> *both to abound and to suffer need. I can do all things through Christ which strengtheneth me. (KJV)*

These verses have always spoken to my heart. I remember writing them on a band-aid as a fourteen-year- old. I had the great honor to go on a mission trip to the countries of Trinidad and Tobago in South America with my church. We helped to build a local church and I remember working with concrete, sanding and scrubbing walls. I remember a family allowing me to use their outhouse; this was a great honor for them. My greatest memory from the trip was the day we went to visit the schools. I stood as a shy teen girl in front of hundreds of children. I held up my band-aid and a bottle of Tylenol and began to share these verses. It is a moment I will never forget because I felt God's calling on my life and I knew I would reach young people in some way. However, it wasn't until I had to live daily by the verses during those dark months that I truly understood their meaning. God had shown me how to abound and to be full in both life and love during many years in my life. Now I was in a different season of my life and I was experiencing emptiness, suffering and need. Just like Paul in Philippians, I had to be content no matter what state my life was currently in, because God would give me the strength to make it through any and all things.

Rejection leaves the deepest and darkest scars in our hearts. It steals our security and our joy in everything we thought was beautiful. It leaves us scared, fragile and more vulnerable than others. But those scars remind us of the One who has carried us through. I refused to let the devil make me a victim of my circumstances. The Lord brought to my mind the Serenity Prayer by Reinhold Niebuhr.

> God grant me the serenity
> to accept the things I cannot change;
> courage to change the things I can;
> and wisdom to know the difference.
>
> Living one day at a time;
> enjoying one moment at a time;
> accepting hardships as the pathway to peace;
> taking, as He did, this sinful world
> as it is, not as I would have it;

> trusting that He will make all things right
> if I surrender to His Will;
> that I may be reasonably happy in this life
> and supremely happy with Him
> forever in the next.
> Amen.[1]

As a child and a young adult, I had only learned the verse of this poem. When I discovered the rest, I was amazed at how the Lord spoke to me. I made it the prayer of my heart.

There will be good days and bad days ahead. When the bad days outnumber the good that is when panic will come creeping in. The panic will start to replace the peace and the uncertainty will begin to overshadow your faith. Discouragement will start to override your joy. It does not mean you are weak, or that your faith is failing. Remember your enemy, the devil, and stand and shout with a mighty voice, "I trust you Lord."

We must praise God for even the smallest thing in our lives. Remember when your children were infants. You would study them intently; watching and waiting for them to reach milestones.

"Look he just smiled at me!"

"I can't believe she just laughed!"

"He squeezed my hand."

If you are both willing, if you are both committed, and most importantly, if you keep Christ in the center of your relationship, then you can rebuild your relationship with your spouse. Baby steps literally; or what I like to call baby moments! I would ask God to show me some small sign from Troy every day to give me hope. Whether it

---

[1] *http://www.beliefnet.com/prayers/protestant/addiction/serenity-prayer.aspx#6Km59LokQLMRLqLT.99*

was an email, a gesture, or a kind word. Granted, I did not get these glimpses or baby steps every day and it has been a constant roller coaster ride. But, when I seemed to be at the end of my rope, about to give up and lose all hope I would beg the Lord to show me something. Every single time I reached this point, He would show me something from Troy. Those baby moments were small victories for me. I got a notebook and started writing down those small moments, so I could "see" God working when the devil tried to discourage me!

☙ JOURNAL ❧

Are you willing to be fully committed to rebuilding your marriage with your spouse? Is your spouse seeking forgiveness, restitution, and willing to rebuild your marriage with you? If you have discussed these things take some time and write down your feelings, fears, or thoughts. What do you think will be the most difficult part of the rebuilding process? Forgiving or rebuilding trust? What do you think are the most important actions you need to help with this process? Counseling? An accountability partner? Acts of trust, like phone calls or knowing a spouses' location at all times? Knowing what you are your spouse are willing to do will help you both determine your willingness to commit to each other?

_____

_____

_____

_____

_____

_____

_____

_____

THE BREAKING AND MAKING OF ME

Gracie Kay

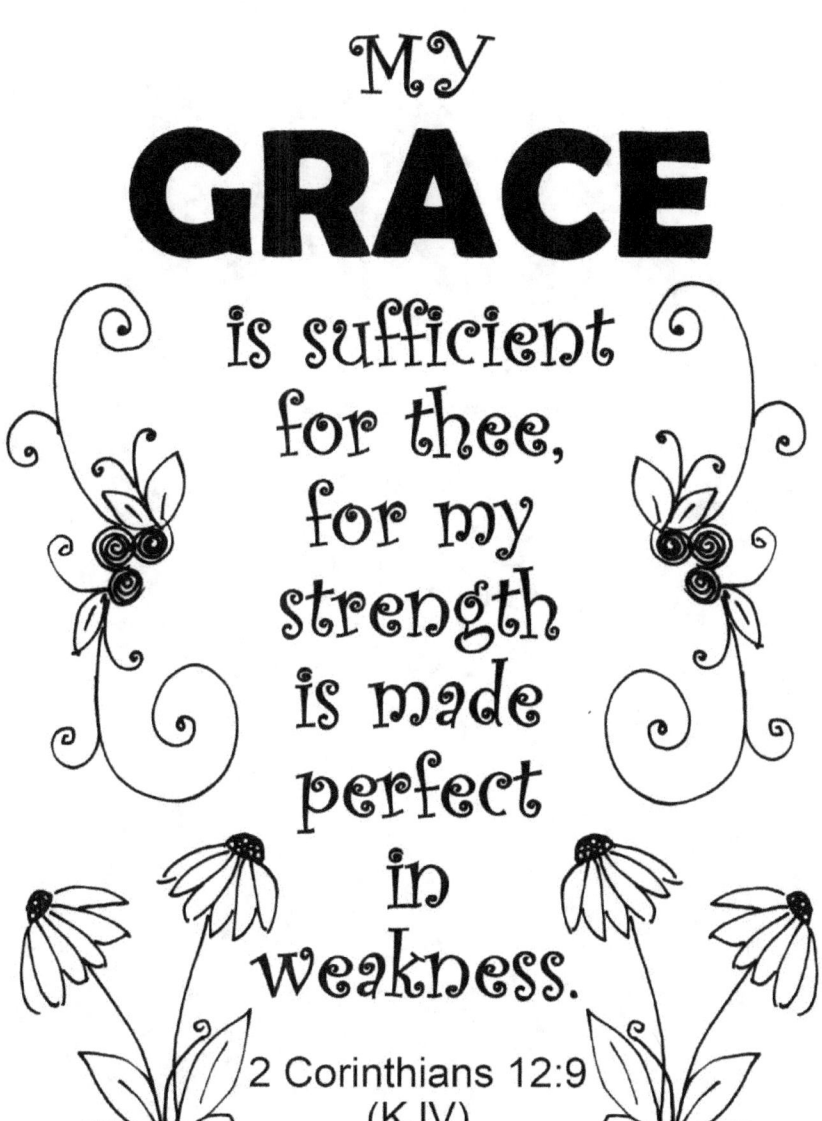

Gracie Kay

STEP NINE

The Future

Remember the song form the 80's with the famous line, "My future's so bright I gotta wear shades"? As corny as it sounds this is how God wants us to think about our future! We must have a vision. If we don't have a vision our lives are pointless. *"Where there is no vision the people perish." Proverbs 29:18 (KJV)*

Throughout this long journey it has been difficult to see hope on the horizon, but I know my hope is in a mighty God who has something beautiful and good waiting on the horizon. I have a future and a purpose, and it is very bright indeed! We must not lose our vision for the future. When we do, it causes us to be overwhelmed and hopeless. God can restore our lost vision. He can give us hope to dream again. He alone can give us assurance of a promising future! He has more waiting for us than we can ever imagine. In 1 Corinthians 2:9, we are reminded that, *"Eye has not seen, nor ear heard, nor have entered into the heart of man the things which God has prepared for those who love Him." (KJV). "There is hope in your future, says the Lord." Jeremiah 31:17 (NKJV)*

I've always had a problem with worry. As a woman, it is only natural to worry about certain things. Will my children develop properly? Will my children be successful in school? Will they make and keep the right kinds of friends? Will they have confidence and be a leader among their peers? Will the medical problems one of my children face continue to be a part of their life each and every day? Will they be happy and protected? I know all the mothers out there have had all of these kinds of worries. The other day when I was doing my devotion God showed me something.

> *Worry...compromises your joy,*
> *cramps your peace, and confines your freedom.*
> *-June Hunt*

I cannot worry about the future. God doesn't want me to know my future, He wants me to know Him. He wants me to trust Him to guide me into the future one step at a time. I know who holds tomorrow and I know who holds my hand; my God.

ஐ **JOURNAL** ☙

What is your vision or dream for the future?

___

___

___

___

___

___

___

___

___

___

___

___

___

___

___

___

___

___

___

___

___

___

___

Gracie Kay

Gracie Kay

CONCLUSION

Like most young, southern girls, I dreamed of marrying my prince charming, having children, and a great big house. Oh, and of course having the perfect career! Although my story has not turned out quite like I planned - hold that thought - nothing like I planned, I am content with the life God has allowed me to live. I choose to find joy in the little things and to see God's hand of grace and mercy each and every day.

I Survived

As a young girl I was scared of tunnels. Every year we would go for a drive on The Blue Ridge Parkway in the mountains of North Carolina. There are a lot of tunnels on the Parkway. Those tunnels seemed so dark and long and I knew there was this massive mountain right over my head just waiting to collapse. A little "Debby Downer" I know, but at least I knew if I kept looking straight ahead I could catch a small glimpse of light. Then all of a sudden, the darkness was behind me and we emerged into the bright sunlight! Through this dark period in my life I kept my eyes on the "Son-light" of Jesus Christ and I emerged on the other side of this tunnel a "stronger" woman in Christ. Of course, there were many days I could not see His light, but I could always feel His love and His strength! He taught me how to bring every thought, every worry and every hurt to Him in prayer. He taught me how to rely on the Holy Spirit's leading and to depend on the Strength of Christ. He taught me how to let go and let Him take control. In short, God taught me how to survive---every second, every minute, every hour. One day at a time and one month at a time!

I Was Revived

My family was always mustang crazy. Crazy about the car, not the horses that is. I grew up around classic cars and car shows. My first two cars were mustangs. In fact, I can still impress my children when I can recognize the sound of a mustang a mile away. The sound of that engine will always stir something inside of me and remind me of my childhood. Through this dark time in my life, God stirred something else inside my heart. Through the utter and complete dependence on Him, a stronger faith and deeper love for Christ emerged. I learned to depend on His strength, rely on His comfort, and expect miracles. A new passion and relationship with the Lord was ignited. I realized the full potential of God's strength living inside of me. The strength, or Holy Spirit, lives inside all who believe. Most of us choose to let it sit idle and unused like an old 1968 mustang inside a dusty barn. Me - I am going to rev up the engine and let all the "horses" out of the barn. The devil does not stand a chance against the power of God! Maybe - just maybe - when I get to Heaven there will be a candy apple red 1968 Mustang convertible waiting for me.

I Am Going to Thrive

To thrive means to prosper or flourish. Orchids are beautiful and delicate plants, but I must say I do not have much of a green thumb. My husband gave me one on a special occasion. It was the most beautiful shade of yellow. I watered it every ten days just like it said. The flowers faded, and I waited for it to bloom again. Nothing happened. Months went by and still nothing happened. I moved it from one location to the next and still nothing. Then one day I realized my mistake. I was not providing the right environment for it to thrive. It needed bright sunlight, but not direct sunlight. I was not thriving as a Christian or reaching my full potential in Christ before this trial came into my life. I needed the right environment for my life and my soul to thrive. I needed to live daily in God's word and communicate with Him through prayer. To be a light for the world so others could learn about Christ through me. To understand that His love and compassion far exceeds my understanding. To believe His will may not be my will but being completely at peace and to know God always has something wonderful waiting for me, just over the horizon.

My story, your story, is far from over. Our journeys have just begun.

Epilogue

After two years and multiple separations my husband and I are a work in progress, but I am okay. I would never willingly live through this "dark time" again, but I am thankful for it. Yes, I know that sounds crazy, but I am a stronger Christian now then I was before. I survived! My faith and My passion in Christ were revived. I am thriving in God's "son light" and learning every day what new purposes God has in store, when I rest completely in His will. Do I know what will happen to us in the future? No. At the conclusion of this book, we are still legally married but have not lived under the same roof for months. We do things as a family and are working on our friendship. We love each other neither and one of us wants to quit. I do not know when my roller coaster ride will end, but whatever happens, I am trusting that God has something wonderful in store for us. Even now, on the really tough days when I don't know what to pray, I simply say this: "God I love you and I know You love me. You have proven your love to me over and over. God you are good. You have been so good to me. I trust you to be God!"

My God is not finished with you or me!

Gracie Kay

ADMIT THAT YOU HAVE SINNED
For all have sinned and fall short of the glory of God. Romans 3:23 (NKJV)

BELIEVE GOD'S PROMISE
For God so loved the world that he gave his only begotten son, that whosoever believeth in him should not perish but have everlasting life. John 3:16 (KJV)

CONFESS YOUR SINS AND ACCEPT THE GIFT OF SALVATION
If you confess with your mouth the Lord Jesus and believe in you heart that God has raised him from the dead, you will be saved. For with the heart one believes unto righteousness, and with the mouth confession is made unto salvation. Romans 10:9-10 (NKJV)

Gracie Kay

ACKNOWLEDGEMENTS

To my Lord and Savior for loving me, for giving me strength, and for reminding me there is always a purpose for everything we face in this life.

To my parents for offering me Godly guidance, love and support.

To my therapist and doctor for helping me along the way with their expertise.

To Ruth Griffin at Studio Griffin, for her knowledge, wisdom, and expert advice.

Without all of these people, I would not be the woman I am today!

Gracie Kay

ABOUT THE AUTHOR

Gracie Kay lives in a small town in North Carolina. She is a wife and mother, whose active kids keep her involved in sports, school, and church activities. Over the last decade, she has been closely involved in nurturing many young children, through her church and her community. She loves writing, reading, singing and helping others as well as creating and shaping things with her hands. Above all else, Gracie desires to help others see the love of Christ, whether it's through her words, or her actions.

Gracie Kay

www.ingramcontent.com/pod-product-compliance
Lightning Source LLC
Chambersburg PA
CBHW071501070526
44578CB00001B/403